THE KITCHEN LIBRARY
FOOD PROCESSOR COOKING

THE KITCHEN LIBRARY

FOOD PROCESSOR COOKING

Wendy Godfrey

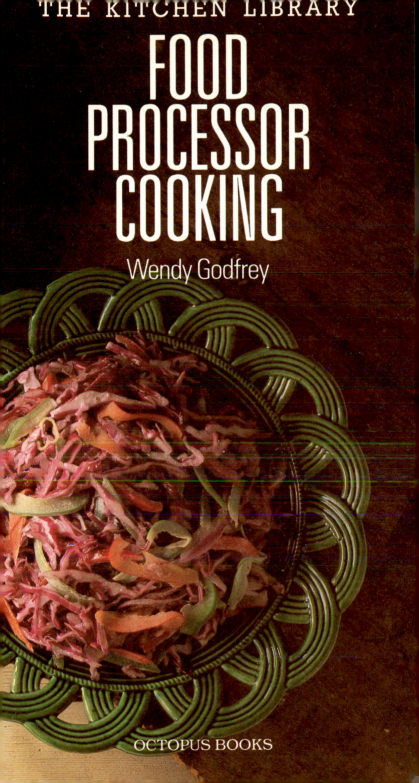

OCTOPUS BOOKS

CONTENTS

This edition published 1986 by
Octopus Books Limited
Michelin House, 81 Fulham Road
London SW3 6RB
Reprinted 1987, 1988, 1990 (twice), 1991

© Cathay Books 1984
ISBN 0 7064 2979 6

Printed by Mandarin Offset in Hong Kong

INTRODUCTION

Of all the electrical food preparation machines that have come onto the market over the last twenty years, the food processor must be the most revolutionary. Its compact size suits it to all modern kitchens, where space is always at a premium, and in that compact space it can perform most of the basic processes needed for preparing food: mixing, 'mincing', shredding, slicing, chopping, liquidizing. Not only this, it performs these processes with such amazing speed that dishes can be prepared in minutes without any physical effort.

Every Kenwood processor has its own particular features and it is essential when using the recipes in this book to follow also the instructions from the individual handbook. This is particularly important from the volume point of view. Some machines can process 500g (1lb 2oz) flour for breadmaking, others 1 Kg (2lb 4oz). Adding more than the machine is designed for will overload the motor and may cause damage. Using more liquid than the machine is designed for will make a mess on your work surface and could also seep into the motor and cause damage.

Use your processor properly and to its fullest potential and you will be amazed at the results. It can help turn even the most inexperienced cook into a veritable *chef de cuisine*.

NOTES

Standard spoon measurements are used in all recipes
1 tablespoon = one 15 ml spoon
1 teaspoon = one 5 ml spoon

Fresh herbs are used unless otherwise stated. If unobtainable substitute a bouquet garni of the equivalent dried herbs, or use dried herbs instead but halve the quantities stated.

Use freshly ground black pepper where pepper is specified.

For all recipes, quantities are given in both metric and imperial measures. Follow either set but not a mixture of both, because they are not interchangeable.

Preparation of ingredients marked with an asterisk is explained on pages 6-11.

USING A FOOD PROCESSOR

All Kenwood processors come with an instruction
manual and basic recipe book, which explain how the
individual machine operates and basic processes like slicing,
grating, blending, etc. The information on these pages is
intended to supplement the handbook, not replace it. It
describes the uses of the three basic attachments and gives
additional information on extra accessories. Preparations of
everyday foods, such as chopped onion, herbs, breadcrumbs,
grated cheese, etc., are explained here in detail and marked
with an asterisk where they occur.

All Kenwood processors are fitted with three accessories: a
metal chopping and mixing blade, a **grating disc** and a
slicing disc. A spatula for scraping down the bowl and
accessories, and a feed tube pusher are also provided.

Other accessories and attachments available are dough
tools, slicing discs with different ranges of slice thickness,
shredding discs, chipping discs, juicing separators, citrus
juicers and egg whisks.

Most machines have at least two speeds and many have a
pulse button. When the pulse button is used, the machine
works in short bursts; this is useful for foods such as cream
or mashed potatoes which are easily spoiled by over
processing.

Usually processes are carried out so quickly that there is no
time to leave the machine and do other jobs. The times given
are a guide only and will vary according to the size of the

processing bowl, speed selected, quantity mixed and
temperature of ingredients.

OTHER ACCESSORIES

Chipping disc: This is used mainly for potatoes, but courgettes
and parsnips can also be processed with this attachment.

Juice separator: This is used for hard fruits and vegetables
which would have a coarse texture if simply puréed with the
metal chopping blade. Apple and carrot juice are very
popular.

Citrus juicer: This is used for extracting the juice from
oranges, lemons, grapefruit and limes.

Egg whisk: The main criticism of the food processor has been
its lack of success in whisking egg whites. All machines will
whisk egg whites and an egg whisk attachment is available
for all Kenwood models to overcome this problem.

METAL CHOPPING BLADE

In general, hard foods should be dropped onto the metal
chopping blade through the feed tube and soft foods should
be placed in the bowl before the motor is started.

Use this attachment for basic cake, scone, bread, batter and
pastry mixes. It will perform sifting, rubbing in, mixing,
whisking, beating, blending and kneading very quickly;
rubbing fat into flour takes 10 to 15 seconds; combining
softened butter and sugar takes 30 seconds; and kneading
dough takes 1 minute. Liquid added to these mixtures can be
poured down the feed tube or sprinkled over the ingredients.
Because all the processing is done by machine, mixtures are
much lighter than if they had been made by hand.

Raw meat: Remove any gristle, bone and excess fat, cut the
meat into 2.5 cm (1 inch) cubes and place in the processor
bowl. Check the coarseness required every 5-10 seconds.

Raw fish: Remove the skin and bones, cut the flesh into
cubes and process as for raw meat.

Cook meat and fish: These process more quickly than the
raw product. Other ingredients, such as vegetables or liquids,
should be mixed with the processed meat or fish by hand to
avoid loss of textures.

Herbs: Wash, dry on kitchen paper and remove any coarse
stalks. Place in the processor bowl and process for 15 seconds.
Process chives and spring onion tops in the same way.
Freshly chopped herbs can be stored in a refrigerator for a
few days or can be frozen.

Onions: Skin and quarter, then place in the processor bowl.
To chop coarsely takes about 3 to 5 seconds; to chop very
finely takes 10-15 seconds.

Mushrooms: Wipe and trim, then process as for onions.

Mashed potatoes: These require careful control. Place a few
cooked potatoes at a time in the processor bowl and process
for 1 to 2 seconds; check the consistency every second, as
they become glutinuous if overprocessed. If your machine
has a pulse button, use it.

Vegetable purée: Place cooked vegetables, such as carrots,
swede, cauliflower, in the processor bowl and process for 15
seconds to form a purée. If liked, add butter or cream to
enrich the mixture, or herbs or spices to flavour.

Soups: Gradually add stock to puréed vegetables through the
feed tube with the machine switched on. Do not over fill.

Soft fruits: Hull the fruit or remove the stalks and place in
the processor bowl. Process for 5 to 10 seconds to a purée.
Stoned mangoes and peaches can be puréed in the same
way.

Hard fruits: Apples, pears, apricots and plums are all
suitable. Remove any stones, stalks, cores, etc., then cook in
a sugar syrup until tender. Drain, place in the processor

bowl and process for 5 to 10 seconds until a purée forms.
Nuts: Remove shells but it is not necessary to skin nuts. Drop
them into the bowl through the feed tube. To chop coarsely
process for 10 to 15 seconds; to grind finely, process for a
further 10 to 20 seconds.

Breadcrumbs, etc: Bread, plain biscuits and cake can be
crumbed. Bread must not be too dry or it will not make fine
crumbs, nor very fresh, as it clings together in a doughy
mass around the blades. Drop bread, biscuits or cake into the
bowl through the feed tube and process for 5 to 10 seconds.

Cheese: To chop hard cheese, cut into 2.5 cm (1 inch) cubes
and drop down the feed tube with the motor on. Check
every 5 seconds until the desired size is achieved.

Vinegar and oil dressings or marinades: Put all the ingredients
in the processor bowl and process for 30 seconds.

Savoury dips: use curd cheese, cream cheese, soured cream
or yogurt as a base and flavour with drained canned tuna or
sardines, crushed pineapple, blue cheese or relishes. Place
the base and flavouring in the bowl and process for 10
seconds.

Savoury butters: Use garlic, curry powder, lemon rind

and juice, chopped herbs or anchovies to taste. Place in the bowl with the butter and process for 10 seconds.

Pastry: Put flour and fat into the bowl, process until the mixture resembles breadcrumbs, take care not to overprocess. Leave the machine on while adding the liquid through the feed tube. Process just until balls of "dough" are formed. If possible chill for 30 minutes before rolling.

Sorbets and ices: Process 2 or 3 times during freezing to break down large crystals and give a smooth textured finish.

Milk shakes: These can be made very quickly. Place the milk in the processor bowl and add fruit, flavouring and sugar to taste. Process for 5 to 10 seconds to blend well. For extra frothiness, add a little ice cream.

SLICING DISC

Only one standard slicing disc, is included with the basic machine. It is most useful to have two slicing thicknesses available and it is worth investing in a second disc. If you do not have a thin slicing disc and a recipe specifies it, don't worry - use the basic disc, as it won't affect the end result too much. Always use the pusher to feed ingredients into the bowl - *never* push down with fingers.

Slicing vegetables for salads: For vegetables which are to be served raw, especially cucumbers and carrots, use a thin slicer. Peel if wished and cut into pieces slightly shorter than the feed tube. Place upright in the tube, switch on the motor and press down lightly with the pusher. Use a similar technique for radishes and mushrooms, piling them into the tube.

Slicing vegetables for cooking: Prepare carrots, celery, courgettes, fennel, onions, and potatoes using a thick slicer if possible. Follow the technique described for thin slicing

vegetables (above).

Potato crisps and game chips: Slice potatoes using the thin slicer before frying.

Leafy vegetables: Red, green and white cabbage, and Chinese leaves, can be shredded before cooking or using in salads. use a standard slicer if possible. Trim and remove the core, cut into pieces small enough to go in the feed tube, switch on the motor and press down lightly with the pusher.

Bananas, apples and pears: Prepare and process as for cucumber. Use on fruit flans, as the slices are all even.

Cheese: Use the thick or thin slicing disc to slice cheese for sandwiches, toasting or pizzas. Cut into pieces to fit into feed tube, switch on motor and press down lightly with the pusher.

GRATING/SHREDDING DISC

One size is usually sufficient for grating purposes, although a fine disc gives a more professional finish to some vegetables for salads and garnishes. Always use the pusher to feed the ingredients into the bowl - *never* the fingers.

Carrots: Peel, cut into pieces, stack neatly in the feed tube, switch on the motor and press down firmly with the pusher. Other crisp vegetables can be grated for use in salads.

Chocolate: Pack upright in the feed tube. Switch on the motor and press down firmly with the pusher. Use to decorate the sides or tops of cakes and desserts.

Hard cooking cheese: Process as for chocolate and use for incorporating into cooked dishes or for gratinées.

Apples: Peel, core and quarter, then process as for chocolate. Use in cakes, desserts and mincemeat.

BASIC RECIPES

Choux Pastry

125 g (4 oz) butter
300 ml (½ pint) water
150 g (5 oz) plain flour, sifted
4 eggs

Place the butter and water in a pan and heat gently until melted, then bring to the boil. Remove from the heat, add the flour all at once and beat well with a wooden spoon. Return to the heat and stir until the mixture leaves the side of the pan.

Fit the metal chopping blade and place the mixture in the processor bowl. Switch on the machine, add the eggs one at a time and process until smooth.

Makes a '4–egg quantity' pastry

VARIATIONS

Cheese Choux: Add 25 g (1 oz) grated Gruyère or Parmesan cheese to the basic mixture and process for 2 to 3 seconds.

Sweet Choux: Add 25 g (1 oz) caster sugar to the butter and water in the pan.

SUGGESTED USES

Profiteroles: Place teaspoonfuls of the basic mixture on a greased baking sheet. Bake in a preheated hot oven, 230°C (450°F), Gas Mark 8, for 10 minutes. Lower heat to 180°C (350°F), Gas Mark 4, and bake for a further 20 minutes. Make a slit in each and return to the oven for 3 minutes. Cool on a wire rack. Fill with whipped cream and top with a warm chocolate sauce. **Serves 6**

Eclairs: Spoon the basic mixture into a piping bag fitted with a 1 cm (½ inch) plain nozzle and pipe into 7.5 cm (3 inch) lengths on a greased baking sheet. Bake as for profiteroles, but allowing 30 minutes at the lower temperature. Cool on a wire rack. Fill with whipped cream and top with coffee glacé icing or melted chocolate. **Makes 20 to 24**

Choux Buns: Place spoonfuls of the sweet choux pastry on a greased baking sheet. Continue as for éclairs. Fill with whipped cream and top with icing sugar to serve. **Makes 20 to 24**

Choux Ring: Spoon the basic mixture into a 23 cm (9 inch) circle on a greased baking sheet. Bake as for profiteroles, but allowing 40 minutes at the lower temperature. Split the cake horizontally and spoon out any uncooked mixture. Return to the oven for 3 minutes to dry out. Cool on a wire rack. Fill with whipped cream and fruit. **Serves 6 to 8**

Cheese Aigrettes: Make up Cheese choux pastry, drop teaspoonfuls of the mixture into hot oil and deep-fry for 3 to 5 minutes, until golden. **Makes 30 to 36**

Shortcrust Pastry

350 g (12 oz) plain
  flour
1/2 teaspoon salt
175 g (6 oz) butter or
  hard margarine
4 tablespoons cold
  water

Fit the metal chopping blade, put the flour and salt in the processor bowl and process for 2 seconds to sift.

Add the fat in small pieces and process for 5 to 10 seconds. Sprinkle the water over the surface and process until the pastry forms a ball around the blade.

Wrap in cling film and chill for 30 minutes before rolling out.

Use as required for tarts, flans, pies, etc.

Makes 350 g (12 oz) pastry

Cheese Pastry

250 g (8 oz) plain
  flour
1/2 teaspoon salt
75 g (3 oz) butter
50 g (2 oz) Cheddar
  cheese, grated*
1 egg yolk
1 tablespoon cold
  water

Fit the metal chopping blade, put the flour and salt in the processor bowl and process for 2 seconds to sift.

Add the butter in pieces and process for 5 to 10 seconds. Stir in the cheese.

Add the egg yolk and water and process until the pastry forms a ball around the blade.

Wrap in cling film and chill for 30 minutes before rolling out.

Use as required for cheese straws, biscuits, flans, etc.

Makes 250 g (8 oz) pastry

Sweet Flan Pastry

250 g (8 oz) plain
  flour
50 g (2 oz) caster or
  icing sugar
125 g (4 oz) butter
2 egg yolks

Fit the metal chopping blade, put the flour and sugar in the processor bowl and process for 2 seconds to sift.

Add the butter in small pieces and process for 5 to 10 seconds.

Add the egg yolks and process until the pastry forms a ball around the blade.

Wrap in cling film and chill for 30 minutes before rolling out.

Use as required for sweet flans and pies, mince tarts, etc.

Makes 250 g (8 oz) pastry

Batter

1 egg
300 ml (½ pint)
  milk, or half milk
  half water mixed
pinch of salt
125 g (4 oz) plain
  flour

Fit the metal chopping blade, place the egg and milk in the processor bowl and process for 3 seconds.

Add the salt and flour down the feed tube and process for 30 seconds.

Use for Yorkshire pudding, toad-in-the-hole and pancakes.

Makes 450 ml (¾ pint)

NOTE: It is not necessary to rest batter before using.

VARIATIONS

Light Batter: Separate the egg. Process yolk with milk, as above. Whisk egg white until firm; fold into the batter.

Coating Batter: Halve the quantity of liquid.

Thin Lacy Crêpes: Process 50 g (2 oz) cooled melted butter with the egg and milk mixture.

Sandwich Cake Mixture

175 g (6 oz) soft tub
  margarine
175 g (6 oz) caster
  sugar
3 eggs
175 g (6 oz) self-
  raising flour
1 tablespoon hot
  water

Fit the metal chopping blade, place all the ingredients in the processor bowl and process until smooth. Divide between 2 lined and greased 18 cm (7 inch) sandwich tins and bake in a preheated moderate oven, 180°C (350°F), Gas Mark 4, for 20 to 25 minutes, until the cakes spring back when lightly pressed. Turn onto a wire rack to cool.

Sandwich together with jam, cream or butter cream and finish with sifted icing sugar or buttercream.
Makes one 18 cm (7 inch) cake

VARIATIONS
Coffee: Replace water with 1 tablespoon coffee essence.
Chocolate: Blend 1 tablespoon cocoa powder with the hot water.
Lemon: Add the grated rind of 1 lemon and 1 tablespoon lemon juice instead of the hot water.
Slab Cake: Place mixture in a lined and greased 30 × 20 cm (12 × 8 inch) cake tin. Bake as above, but for 30 minutes, and cool on a wire rack. Decorate as liked and cut into 12 squares.

Bread Dough

2 teaspoons dried
  yeast
300 ml (½ pint)
  warm water
½ teaspoon sugar
500 g (1 lb) strong
  white plain flour
2 teaspoons salt

Mix yeast with the water and sugar; leave for 10 minutes. Fit the metal chopping blade and put the flour and salt in the bowl. With the machine on, add the yeast mixture through the feed tube. Process for 1 minute, then place in a large oiled polythene bag. Leave to rise in a warm place for about 1½ hours, until doubled in size.

Turn onto a floured surface and knead lightly to remove air bubbles, then process for 15 seconds. Shape into loaves and place in 2 greased 500 g (1 lb) loaf tins, or into rolls and place on greased baking sheets. Leave in a warm place to 'prove' for 30 minutes.

Bake in a preheated hot oven, 230°C (450°F), Gas Mark 8, for 30 minutes for the loaves, 10 minutes for the rolls. Cool on a wire rack.
Makes 2 loaves or 16 rolls

VARIATIONS
Rich Dough: Add 50 g (2 oz) white vegetable fat to the bowl with the flour and salt and process for 5 seconds.
Brown Bread: Replace plain flour with wheatmeal flour.

SOUPS, SAUCES & DIPS

Quick French Onion Soup

500 g (1 lb) onions
50 g (2 oz) butter
1 × 425 g (15 oz)
  can consommé
450 ml (¾ pint)
  water
1 tablespoon beef
  extract
6 thick slices French
  bread
75 g (3 oz) Cheddar
  cheese, grated*
3 tablespoons brandy
  (optional)

Fit the slicing disc and slice the onions.

Melt the butter in a pan, add the onions and fry until a rich brown. Add the consommé, water and beef extract and bring to simmering point.

Toast the French bread on both sides and top with the grated cheese. Toast until the cheese is bubbling.

Add the brandy to the soup, if using, and ladle into individual soup bowls. Add the toasted bread slices.
Serves 6

Cheese and Celery Soup

2 onions
1 head of celery
50 g (2 oz) butter
1.2 litres (2 pints)
  water
2 chicken stock cubes
1/2 teaspoon grated
  nutmeg
salt and pepper
125 g (4 oz) blue
  cheese, chopped*

Fit the metal chopping blade and process the onions. Reserve a few celery leaves for garnish, then process the celery.

Melt the butter in a large pan, add the onion and celery and fry gently until softened. Add 300 ml (1/2 pint) of the water and simmer for 1 hour.

Process until smooth, then return to the pan and stir in the remaining water and the stock cubes. Add the nutmeg, and salt and pepper to taste. Bring to simmering point and stir in the cheese.

Transfer the soup to warmed bowls. Garnish with the reserved celery leaves and serve immediately.
Serves 4 to 6

Smoked Haddock Soup

350 g (12 oz)
  smoked haddock
450 ml (¾ pint)
  water
1 onion
50 g (2 oz)
  mushrooms
50 g (2 oz) butter
1 teaspoon curry
  powder
50 g (2 oz) plain
  flour
600 ml (1 pint) milk
pepper
2 tablespoons dry
  sherry

Poach the haddock in the water for 10 minutes; set aside. Reserve 300 ml (½ pint) of the cooking liquor.

Fit the metal chopping blade and chop the onion and mushrooms together coarsely. Melt the butter in a large pan, add the onion, mushrooms and curry powder and fry for 5 minutes. Stir in the flour and gradually add the milk and reserved liquor.

Remove the skin from the cooked haddock, place the fish in the processor bowl and chop roughly. Add to the soup and heat through gently. Season with pepper to taste.

Pour into a serving bowl and stir in the sherry to serve.
Serves 6

Fish Soup with Rouille

1 large onion
2 cloves garlic
2 tablespoons olive
  oil
250 g (8 oz)
  tomatoes, skinned
1 litre (1¾ pints)
  water
2 whiting fillets,
  skinned
250 g (8 oz) monk
  fish, cubed
bouquet garni
salt and pepper
ROUILLE:
1 thick slice French
  bread, crust
  removed
2 cloves garlic
2 red peppers, cored
  and seeded
2 tablespoons olive
  oil
TO SERVE:
French bread slices

Fit the metal chopping blade and roughly chop the onion and garlic. Heat the oil in a large pan, add the onion and garlic and fry until browned.

Roughly chop the tomatoes and add to the pan with the water. Chop the whiting and add to the soup with the monk fish, bouquet garni, and salt and pepper to taste. Bring to the boil and simmer for 20 minutes.

Meanwhile, make the rouille. Soak the bread in water to cover until soft.

Using the metal chopping blade, process the garlic and peppers until smooth. Squeeze the bread, add to the processor bowl with the oil and process, adding enough liquor from the soup to make a thick sauce. Pour into a serving bowl.

Toast the French bread and put a slice in the bottom of individual soup bowls. Ladle the soup over the toast and top with a spoonful of rouille.
Serves 6 to 8

Carrot and Coriander Soup

1 onion
1 clove garlic
25 g (1 oz) butter
25 g (1 oz) plain
　flour
1.2 litres (2 pints)
　chicken stock
500 g (1 lb) carrots
2 teaspoons ground
　coriander
150 g (5.2 oz)
　natural yogurt
salt and pepper
coriander leaves to
　garnish

Fit the metal chopping blade and process the onion and garlic finely. Melt the butter in a large pan, add the onion and garlic and fry until soft. Stir in the flour and gradually add the stock, stirring until thickened.

Fit the grating disc and grate the carrots. Add to the pan with the ground coriander and simmer for 30 minutes.

Fit the metal chopping blade and process the soup in batches. Pour into a clean pan, add the yogurt, and salt and pepper to taste and bring to just below boiling point.

Garnish with coriander to serve.
Serves 6

Lettuce and Watercress Soup

1 onion
25 g (1 oz) butter
1 large potato
900 ml (1½ pints)
    water
2 chicken stock cubes,
    crumbled
1 round lettuce
1 bunch of watercress
salt and pepper
142 ml (5 fl oz)
    single cream
chopped chives or
    spring onion tops*
    to garnish

Fit the metal chopping blade and chop the onion roughly. Melt the butter in a pan, add the onion and fry gently.

Chop the potato roughly, add to the pan and cook for 2 minutes. Add the water and stock cubes, bring to the boil and simmer for 15 minutes.

Tear the lettuce into small pieces and add to the pan with the watercress. Bring to the boil, then remove from the heat.

Process in 3 or 4 batches and pour into a serving bowl. Season with salt and pepper to taste and leave to cool. Chill in the refrigerator until required.

Stir in the cream and sprinkle with chives or spring onion tops to serve.
Serves 4 to 6
NOTE: Crunchy lettuces are not suitable for this recipe.

Yogurt and Cucumber Soup

1 cucumber, peeled
salt and pepper
500 g (1 lb) natural
   yogurt
142 ml (5 fl oz)
   soured cream
300 ml (½ pint)
   water
6 mint sprigs,
   chopped*
TO GARNISH:
½ teaspoon paprika
25 g (1 oz) sultanas
   (optional)

Fit the metal chopping blade and chop the cucumber roughly. Sprinkle with salt and leave to drain.

Place the yogurt, soured cream and water in the processor bowl and blend until smooth. Stir in the mint and cucumber and season liberally with salt and pepper. Transfer to a serving bowl and chill until required.

Sprinkle with the paprika, and sultanas if using, to serve.

Serves 6

Cold Beetroot Soup

350 g (12 oz)
   beetroot, cooked
142 ml (5 fl oz)
   soured cream
600 ml (1 pint)
   chicken stock

Fit the metal chopping blade, put the beetroot and half the soured cream in the processor bowl and process until smooth. Transfer to a bowl and stir in the chicken stock. Chill well.

Pour into individual bowls and stir in the remaining soured cream.

Serves 4 to 6

Mayonnaise

2 egg yolks
2 teaspoons Dijon
   mustard
300 ml (½ pint)
   olive oil, or 150 ml
   (¼ pint) each
   olive and
   sunflower oil
1 tablespoon vinegar
salt and pepper

Fit the metal blade, place the egg yolks, mustard and 1 tablespoon oil in the processor bowl and process for 5 seconds. Dribble the remaining oil through the feed tube with the motor running. When all the oil has been amalgamated, turn off the motor.

Add the vinegar, and salt and pepper to taste, and process again for 3 seconds.

Makes 300 ml (½ pint)

NOTE: All the ingredients must be at room temperature. If the mixture should curdle, switch off the machine and transfer the curdled mixture to a jug or basin. Put another egg yolk in the processor bowl and gradually pour in the curdled mixture, then the remaining oil.

VARIATIONS

Mild Mayonnaise: Add 284 ml (½ pint) double cream, whipped, or 300 g (10.4 oz) natural yogurt to the prepared mayonnaise.

Garlic Mayonnaise: Add 2 cloves garlic to the processor bowl with the egg yolks, mustard and 1 tablespoon oil.

Tomato Mayonnaise: Add 2 tablespoons tomato purée to the prepared mayonnaise, stirring well to blend.

Lemon Mayonnaise: Replace vinegar with lemon juice.

Curry Mayonnaise: Add 1 teaspoon curry powder to the prepared mayonnaise.

Spinach or Watercress Mayonnaise: Add 2 tablespoons spinach or watercress purée to the prepared mayonnaise.

Tartare Sauce: Fit the metal chopping blade and place 1 tablespoon capers, 2 gherkins, 2 to 3 parsley sprigs and ½ onion in the processor bowl. Chop coarsely and stir into the prepared mayonnaise.

Rémoulade Sauce: Fit the metal chopping blade. Place 1 tablespoon capers, 2 gherkins, 2 to 3 parsley sprigs and 1 anchovy fillet in the processor bowl and chop coarsely. Add to the prepared mayonnaise with 1 teaspoon Dijon mustard and stir well to blend.

SUGGESTED USES

Use mayonnaise to bind cooked egg yolks for stuffed eggs.
Use as a coating for cold poached salmon.
Toss prawns in mayonnaise and use for prawn cocktail or as a filling for avocado.

Crème Patissière

50 g (2 oz) caster
  sugar
3 egg yolks
2 tablespoons plain
  flour
2 tablespoons
  cornflour
300 ml (½ pint)
  milk
few drops of vanilla
  essence

Fit the metal chopping blade, place
the sugar and egg yolks in the
processor bowl and process until
pale. Add the flour and cornflour and
process for a few seconds.

Boil the milk and add to the bowl
while the processor is in motion.
Transfer to a pan and heat, stirring
constantly, until thickened. Beat in
the vanilla essence and leave to cool.

Use as a filling for cakes and sweet
pastries, such as vanilla slices and
choux buns.

Makes 450 ml (¾ pint)
NOTE: This can be stored in the
refrigerator for 1 week.

Brandy Butter

125 g (4 oz) unsalted
  butter, cut into
  pieces
350 g (12 oz) soft
  light brown sugar
grated rind of 1
  orange
120 ml (4 fl oz)
  brandy

Fit the metal chopping blade, place
the butter, sugar and orange rind in
the processor bowl and process until
pale and soft. Gradually add the
brandy while the machine is on.

Transfer to a small dish, cover and
store in the refrigerator.

Serve with Christmas Pudding and
hot mince pies, or other hot puddings.
Makes about 500 g (1 lb)

VARIATION
Rum Butter: Replace the light brown sugar and brandy
with muscovado sugar and rum.

Raspberry Sauce

250 g (8 oz)
  raspberries
25 g (1 oz) caster
  sugar
3 tablespoons white
  wine

Fit the metal chopping blade, place
the ingredients in the processor bowl
and blend until smooth.

Serve warm or cold with fresh or
grilled peaches or ice cream, or
chilled with Strawberry Mousse (see
page 73).
Makes 300 ml (½ pint)

Prune and Nut Sauce

125 g (4 oz) walnuts
125 g (4 oz) pitted
  prunes
150 ml (¼ pint) port
  (approximately)
1 teaspoon cinnamon

Fit the metal chopping blade and chop the walnuts roughly; set aside.

Place the prunes, port and cinnamon in a pan and simmer for 10 minutes. Process until smooth, then stir in the walnuts. Thin the sauce to the desired consistency by adding more port.

Serve with roast pork, grilled pork chops or turkey.

Makes about 450 ml (¾ pint)

Tomato and Orange Sauce

1 bunch of spring
  onions
2 tablespoons oil
500 g (1 lb)
  tomatoes, skinned
juice of 1 orange
1 tablespoon lemon
  juice
2 tablespoons tomato
  purée
salt and pepper

Fit the metal chopping blade and chop the spring onions. Heat 1 tablespoon of the oil in a pan, add the spring onions and fry gently for 2 minutes. Drain well.

Process the tomatoes and gradually add the onions, fruit juices, tomato purée and remaining oil while the machine is running.

Transfer to a serving bowl and season with salt and pepper to taste. Chill well. Serve with fried fish.

Makes about 450 ml (¾ pint)

Cold Curry Sauce

1 egg yolk
½ teaspoon turmeric
¼ teaspoon ground
  cumin
¼ teaspoon ground
  coriander
150 ml (¼ pint)
  sunflower oil
1 tablespoon lemon
  juice
150 g (5.2 oz)
  natural yogurt
salt and pepper

Fit the metal chopping blade, place the egg yolk and spices in the processor bowl and blend for a few seconds. With the machine on, drip in the oil very slowly. Switch off. Add the lemon juice and yogurt and blend for 5 to 10 seconds. Season with salt and pepper to taste.

This light mayonnaise–type sauce is excellent served with salmon or cold chicken.
Makes 300 ml (½ pint)

Herb Butter Sauce

142 ml (5 fl oz)
  double cream
75 g (3 oz) unsalted
  butter
juice of 1 lime or
  lemon
2-3 tarragon sprigs,
  chopped*
2-3 chives, chopped*
salt
paprika

Fit the metal chopping blade. Heat the cream almost to boiling point and pour into the processor bowl. Switch on the machine, add the butter in pieces and gradually pour in the lime or lemon juice. Stir in the tarragon and chives and season with salt and paprika to taste.

Serve with plainly grilled white fish or shellfish.
Makes about 250 ml (8 fl oz)

Kidney Bean Dip

1 × 425 g (15 oz)
   can kidney beans,
   drained and rinsed
2 tablespoons lemon
   juice
6 tablespoons olive
   oil
salt and pepper
3 rashers streaky
   bacon, derinded

Fit the metal chopping blade and place the kidney beans, lemon juice, oil, and salt and pepper to taste in the processor bowl. Process until smooth, then transfer to a serving dish.

Grill the bacon until crisp and golden, then crumble over the top.

Serve with pitta bread or julienne strips of crisp vegetables, such as carrots, cucumber, peppers.
Makes 450 ml (¾ pint)

Tandoori Baste

1 onion
6 cloves garlic
1 small piece fresh
   root ginger, peeled
1 green chilli, seeded
juice of 1 lemon
1 teaspoon each
   ground coriander
   and cumin
2 teaspoons paprika
150 g (5.2 oz)
   natural yogurt
salt and pepper

Fit the metal chopping blade and place all the ingredients, with salt and pepper to taste, in the processor bowl. Process until smooth.

This baste is suitable for use with chicken portions, lamb chops, kebabs of cubed chicken breast, lamb or liver. Marinate the meat in the sauce for 2 hours, then use to baste frequently while grilling.
Makes 200 ml (6 fl oz)

Baba Ghanoush

1 large or 2 small
   aubergines
4 cloves garlic
4 tablespoons tahina
   (sesame seed paste
   – see below)
1 lemon
salt
TO SERVE:
2-3 parsley sprigs,
   chopped*
1 packet pitta bread to
   serve

Prick the aubergines all over and grill, turning frequently, until the skin is charred all over. Remove the skin, rinsing in cold water.

Fit the metal chopping blade. Place the aubergines and remaining ingredients in the processor bowl, seasoning with salt to taste. Process until smooth, then transfer to a serving dish.

Sprinkle with the parsley and serve as a dip with pitta bread.
Makes about 200 ml (⅓ pint)
NOTE: Tahina is available from health food stores and delicatessens.

PÂTÉS & TERRINES

Smoked Mackerel Pâté

4 × 175 g (6 oz)
   smoked mackerel
   fillets, skinned
125 g (4 oz) unsalted
   butter, softened
1 tablespoon
   horseradish sauce
finely grated rind and
   juice of 1 lemon
TO GARNISH:
6 lemon slices, halved
parsley sprigs

Fit the metal chopping blade, place the mackerel, butter, horseradish sauce, lemon rind and juice in the processor bowl and blend for 1 minute. Transfer to 6 individual serving dishes and garnish each with lemon slices and parsley sprigs. Serve with crispbread or toast.
Serves 6

Mushroom Pâté

350 g (12 oz)
  mushrooms
1 onion
125 g (4 oz) butter
4 tablespoons sherry
salt and pepper
parsley sprig to
  garnish

Fit the metal chopping blade and chop the mushrooms and onion. Melt half the butter in a small pan, add the vegetables and fry gently for a few minutes to soften. Stir in the sherry and cook, stirring, until all the liquid has evaporated. Season with salt and pepper to taste and leave until cold.

Place in the processor bowl with the remaining butter and process until smooth.

Spoon into a dish and garnish with parsley. Serve with toast.
Serves 4

Tuna Pâté

2 × 198 g (7 oz) cans
    tuna fish, drained
250 g (8 oz) unsalted
    butter, softened
25 g (1 oz) stoned
    green olives
pepper
TO GARNISH:
lemon slices
parsley sprigs

Fit the metal chopping blade and place all the ingredients in the processor bowl, adding pepper to taste. Process until smooth, transfer to a 900 ml (1½ pint) dish and chill for about 2 hours, or until required.

Serve, garnished with lemon slices and parsley sprigs, accompanied by wholemeal toast.

Serves 4 to 6

Turkey Liver Pâté

1 onion
1 clove garlic
125 g (4 oz) butter
1 × 227 g (8 oz) tub
    frozen turkey
    livers, thawed and
    trimmed
1 tablespoon sweet
    sherry
50 g (2 oz) shelled
    pistachio nuts,
    coarsely chopped*
salt and pepper
watercress sprigs to
    garnish

Fit the metal chopping blade and chop the onion and garlic roughly; set aside.

Melt 75 g (3 oz) of the butter in a small pan, add the turkey livers and fry for 5 minutes, turning frequently. Put in the processor bowl. Fry the onion and garlic in the fat remaining in the pan until softened; add to the bowl.

Melt the remaining butter in the pan and stir in the sherry, scraping up the sediment. Add to the bowl and process until smooth. Stir in the nuts, and salt and pepper to taste.

Transfer to a dish, cover and leave to mature in the refrigerator for 2 days. Garnish with watercress and serve with wholewheat toast.

Serves 4

Garbanzos Pâté

1 × 400 g (14 oz)
    can chick peas,
    drained
125 g (4 oz) salami
2 cloves garlic
salt and pepper
4-6 basil or parsley
    sprigs, chopped*

Fit the metal chopping blade, place the chick peas in the processor bowl and process. Transfer to a mixing bowl. Process the salami and garlic then add to the peas. Season well with salt and pepper and stir in half of the basil or parsley.

Transfer to individual dishes and chill until required.

Garnish with remaining herbs and serve with toast or warm pitta bread.

Serves 4

Duck and Cranberry Terrine

3 duck portions,
  skinned
500 g (1 lb) pork
  fillet
250 g (8 oz) pork
  belly rashers
3 tablespoons brandy
1 egg, beaten
1 teaspoon cinnamon
½ teaspoon grated
  nutmeg
¼ teaspoon salt
¼ teaspoon pepper
50 g (2 oz) fresh or
  frozen cranberries
watercress sprigs to
  garnish

Remove as much flesh from the duck portions as possible. Fit the metal chopping blade and chop the flesh. Place in a mixing bowl.

Chop the pork fillet, then the pork rashers and add to the mixing bowl. Add the remaining ingredients and mix well. Leave to stand for 1 hour.

Transfer to a 1 kg (2 lb) loaf tin or terrine and cook in a preheated moderate oven, 180°C (350°F), Gas Mark 4, for 1 hour. Place weights on top to press down while cooling. Chill for 24 hours to mature.

Garnish with watercress sprigs and serve with crusty bread.

Serves 6

Three–Fish Terrine

500 g (1 lb) plaice
  fillets, skinned
350 g (12 oz)
  smoked haddock,
  skinned
150 g (5.2 oz)
  natural yogurt
2 eggs
grated rind and juice
  of 1 lemon
250 g (8 oz) smoked
  cods' roe
1 tablespoon tomato
  purée
white pepper
TO GARNISH:
lemon slices
parsley sprigs

Line a 1 kg (2 lb) loaf tin or terrine with most of the plaice fillets, skinned side inwards.

Fit the metal chopping blade and place the haddock, 7 tablespoons of the yogurt, 1 egg and the lemon rind and juice in the processor bowl. Process until smooth, then place half the mixture in the terrine.

Process the cods' roe with the remaining yogurt, tomato purée and the yolk of the remaining egg. Whisk the egg white until stiff and fold in. Spoon into the terrine and season with pepper. Spoon the remaining haddock mixture over, and cover with the remaining plaice fillets.

Cover with a lid or foil and place in a roasting pan half-filled with water. Cook in a preheated moderate oven, 180°C (350°F), Gas Mark 4, for 1 hour. Leave to cool.

Pour off any juices and turn onto a serving plate. Garnish with lemon slices and parsley sprigs to serve.

Serves 6 to 8

Chicken and Vegetable Terrine

125 g (4 oz) cooked
   chicken
350 g (12 oz)
   skimmed milk soft
   cheese
3 eggs
salt and white pepper
125 g (4 oz) spinach,
   cooked
125 g (4 oz) carrots,
   cooked
TO SERVE:
Tomato and orange
   sauce (see page 28)
few chives, chopped

Fit the metal chopping blade and
place the chicken, one third of the
cheese and 1 egg in the processor
bowl. Process until a purée forms.
Season with salt and pepper to taste.

Repeat this process twice, using
the spinach, then the carrots, in place
of the chicken.

Grease a 500 g (1 lb) loaf tin and
spoon in the chicken mixture.
Carefully spoon over the carrot
mixture, then the spinach mixture.

Place the tin in a roasting pan
half-filled with water and cook in a
preheated moderate oven, 160°C
(325°F), Gas Mark 3, for 1 hour.

Leave to cool, then turn out onto a
serving plate and surround with the
Tomato and orange sauce, sprinkled
with chives.
Serves 6

Ham Mould

350 g (12 oz) cooked
  lean ham
300 ml (½ pint)
  mayonnaise (see
  page 24)
1 envelope gelatine
4 tablespoons very
  hot water
142 ml (5 fl oz)
  single cream
1 tablespoon Meaux
  mustard
2-3 parsley sprigs,
  chopped*
cucumber slices, to
  garnish

Fit the metal chopping blade, place
the ham in the processor bowl and
chop finely. Add the mayonnaise and
blend for 5 seconds.

Sprinkle the gelatine onto the hot
water and stir until dissolved. Add to
the ham mixture with the remaining
ingredients and blend together
gently.

Transfer to a 1 litre (1¾ pint)
soufflé dish or 4 ramekins and chill
for about 2 hours or until set.

Turn out onto a serving dish and
garnish with the cucumber slices.
Serve with toast.
Serves 4

Game Terrine

18 juniper berries
6 bay leaves
350 g (12 oz) streaky
  bacon, derinded
500 g (1 lb) lean
  venison
500 g (1 lb) stewing
  veal
500 g (1 lb) belly
  pork
2 eggs, beaten
125 g (4 oz) fresh
  breadcrumbs*
1 onion
2 cloves garlic
2 tablespoons oil
1 teaspoon mixed
  herbs
salt and pepper

Arrange 6 juniper berries and the bay leaves in the base of a buttered 1 kg (2lb) loaf tin or terrine to form a flower. Line the base and sides with bacon.

Fit the metal chopping blade, place the venison and remaining juniper berries in the processor bowl and process until finely chopped. Transfer to a mixing bowl. Process the veal and pork together in the same way and add to the mixing bowl with the eggs and breadcrumbs.

Roughly chop the onion and garlic. Heat the oil in a pan, add the onion and garlic and fry gently until softened. Process again and add to the mixing bowl with the herbs, and salt and pepper to taste; mix well.

Transfer to the loaf tin or terrine, pressing down well, and cover with the remaining bacon. Cover with foil and place in a roasting pan half-filled with water. Cook in a preheated moderate oven, 180°C (350°F), Gas Mark 4, for 2 hours.

Leave in the tin and place weights on top to press while cooling. Turn out when cold. Serve with toast.
Serves 8 to 12

Chicken Liver Mousse

50 g (2 oz) butter
1 × 227 g (8 oz) tub
  frozen chicken
  livers, thawed and
  trimmed
50 g (2 oz) button
  mushrooms
1 clove garlic
3 tablespoons sweet
  sherry
salt and pepper
142 ml (5 fl oz)
  double cream,
  whipped

Melt the butter in a small pan, add the livers and mushrooms and fry until the livers turn brown.

Fit the metal chopping blade, place the livers, mushrooms, garlic and sherry in the processor bowl and process until smooth. Season with salt and pepper to taste and add the cream. Process for a further 5 to 10 seconds. Turn into a serving bowl and chill for 2 hours or until required.

Serve with crusty bread.
Serves 4

Veal and Spinach Loaf

500 g (1 lb) spinach
500 g (1 lb) stewing
   veal
125 g (4 oz) ham
1 onion
75 g (3 oz) grated
   Parmesan cheese
2 eggs, beaten
25 g (1 oz) fresh
   breadcrumbs*
parsley sprigs to
   garnish

Cook the spinach gently, with just the water clinging to the leaves after washing, for 5 minutes; drain well.

Fit the metal chopping blade and place the veal, ham and onion in the processor bowl. Chop finely, then transfer to a mixing bowl.

Process the spinach for 5 seconds and add to the mixing bowl.

Add the grated Parmesan cheese to the mixing bowl with the eggs and breadcrumbs; mix well.

Transfer to a greased 1 kg (2 lb) loaf tin or terrine and cook in a preheated moderate oven, 160°C (325°F), Gas Mark 3, for 1 hour.

Turn out and serve sliced, hot or cold. Garnish with parsley sprigs.
Serves 6

Ballotine of Pork

1 pork fillet,
    weighing about
    350 g (12 oz)
350 g (12 oz) pork
    sausage meat
125 g (4 oz) pigs'
    liver
1 tablespoon green
    peppercorns
    (crushed)
1 onion
25 g (1 oz) fresh
    breadcrumbs*
2-3 parsley sprigs,
    chopped*
salt and pepper
watercress sprigs to
    garnish

Cut the fillet almost in half lengthways. Open out and beat thinly between 2 sheets of greaseproof paper. Put the sausage meat in a bowl.

Fit the metal chopping blade, place the liver, peppercorns and onion in the processor bowl and process until smooth. Add to the sausage meat.

Stir in the remaining ingredients, with salt and pepper to taste, and mix well. Shape into one sausage as long as the width of the pork fillet. Place on one end of the fillet and roll up. Fasten with wooden cocktail sticks.

Place in a small baking dish and cover with buttered foil. Cook in a preheated moderate oven, 180°C (350°F), Gas Mark 4, for 1 hour. Drain off any fat and leave until cold.

Chill for at least 3 hours. Slice and garnish with watercress to serve.
Serves 4

Potted Cheese

25 g (1 oz) sultanas
2 tablespoons dry
   sherry
250 g (8 oz)
   farmhouse
   Cheddar cheese
125 g (4 oz) butter
pepper

Soak the sultanas in the sherry for
45 minutes until plump.

Fit the metal chopping blade and
chop the cheese. Add 50 g (2 oz) of
the butter and process until blended.

Stir in the sultanas and sherry and
season to taste with pepper. Spoon
into individual dishes.

Melt the remaining butter and
pour over the potted cheese. Chill for
1 hour or until required. Serve with
hot toast or salad.
Serves 4

Potted Beef

250 g (8 oz) cooked
   lean beef
125 g (4 oz) butter
2 teaspoons Meaux
   mustard
1 tablespoon port
salt and pepper

Fit the metal chopping blade, place
the beef in the processor bowl and
chop finely. Add half the butter to the
bowl and process again until blended.
Stir in the mustard, port, and salt and
pepper to taste. Pack into individual
dishes.

Melt the remaining butter and
pour over the potted beef. Chill for
1 hour or until required. Serve with
hot toast or salad.
Serves 4

Parma Roulade

250 g (8 oz) Parma
   or other smoked
   ham
227 g (8 oz) cream
   cheese
2-3 parsley sprigs,
   chopped*
pepper

Trim the slices of ham to neat
rectangles. Fit the metal chopping
blade, place the ham trimmings in the
processor bowl and chop finely. Add
the cream cheese and parsley and
blend well. Season with pepper to
taste.

Roll into sausage shapes as long as
the width of the ham slices. Place a
cheese roll at one end of each ham
slice and roll up. Cover and chill for
2 hours.

Serve accompanied by slices of
melon, pear or figs, as a starter.
Serves 4

VEGETABLE DISHES & SALADS

Fennel au Gratin

2 fennel bulbs
salt
25 g (1 oz) butter
25 g (1 oz) plain
  flour
150 ml (¼ pint)
  milk
1 teaspoon Meaux
  mustard
75 g (3 oz) Cheddar
  cheese, grated*
1 tablespoon
  breadcrumbs,
  browned*

Fit the slicing disc and slice the fennel.
Cook in boiling salted water for 5
minutes. Drain, reserving 150 ml
(¼ pint) of the cooking liquor.

Melt the butter in a small pan and
stir in the flour. Add the milk
gradually, stirring constantly, and
pour in the reserved stock. Simmer
for 2 minutes, then stir in the mustard
and all but 2 tablespoons of the
cheese. Place the fennel in an
ovenproof dish and pour over the
sauce.

Sprinkle with the remaining cheese
and the breadcrumbs and place under
a preheated hot grill until browned.
Serve immediately.
Serves 4

Broccoli Soufflé

375 g (12 oz)
  broccoli
salt and pepper
25 g (1 oz) butter
25 g (1 oz) plain
  flour
150 ml (¼ pint)
  milk
4 eggs, separated

Cook the broccoli in boiling salted water for 10 minutes; drain. Fit the metal chopping blade, put the broccoli in the bowl and process for 10 seconds.

Melt the butter in a pan and stir in the flour to make a roux. Gradually stir in the milk. Bring to the boil, stirring, and cook until very thick. Cool slightly. Add the egg yolks, broccoli, and salt and pepper to taste. Whisk the egg whites until stiff, then fold into the mixture.

Pour into a buttered 1.2 litre (2 pint) soufflé dish and bake in a preheated moderate oven, 180°C (350°F), Gas Mark 4, for 1 hour. Serve immediately.
Serves 4

Mixed Stir-Fry

1 onion
2 cloves garlic
2.5 cm (1 inch) piece
    fresh root ginger,
    peeled
175 g (6 oz) carrots
175 g (6 oz) white
    cabbage
4 celery sticks
4 tablespoons
    sunflower oil
125 g (4 oz) bean
    sprouts
2 teaspoons soy sauce
2 teaspoons vinegar
1 teaspoon caster
    sugar
salt and pepper

Fit the metal chopping blade, place the onion, garlic and ginger in the processor bowl and process until finely chopped.

Fit the slicing disc and slice the carrots, cabbage and celery separately.

Heat the oil in a large frying pan or wok and add the onion mixture. Stir-fry for 1 minute.

Add the carrots and stir-fry for a further minute. Add the remaining vegetables and stir-fry for 3 minutes.

Sprinkle with the soy sauce, vinegar and sugar, season well with salt and pepper and stir together for 1 minute. Serve immediately.

Serves 6

Aubergine Fritters

3 aubergines
1 tablespoon salt
125 g (4 oz) plain
    flour
1 egg
150 ml (¼ pint)
    milk
1 teaspoon garam
    masala
oil for deep-frying

Fit the slicing disc and slice the aubergines. Sprinkle with the salt and leave to drain for 30 minutes.

Fit the metal chopping blade, place the flour, egg, milk and garam masala in the processor bowl and process for 30 seconds.

Rinse the aubergine slices and pat dry with kitchen paper. Coat each slice in the prepared batter and deep-fry for 8 to 10 minutes, until crisp and golden. Drain on kitchen paper and serve immediately.

Serves 4

NOTE: Long thin aubergines are preferable to rounder ones because they can be sliced into neat rings and do not have to be split to pass through the feed tube.

Rumbledethumps

A traditional Scottish dish which can be served as a vegetable or as a supper dish on its own.

500 g (1 lb) cabbage
salt
1 onion
750 g (1½ lb)
   potatoes, boiled
   and mashed*
125 g (4 oz)
   Cheddar cheese,
   grated*

Fit the slicing disc and shred the cabbage. Cook in a little boiling salted water for 5 minutes; drain.

Fit the metal chopping blade and chop the onion. Mix all the vegetables together and turn into a well buttered 1.2 litre (2 pint) ovenproof dish.

Cover with the cheese and bake in a preheated moderately hot oven, 200°C (400°F), Gas Mark 6, for 20 to 25 minutes, until golden. Serve immediately.

Serves 4 to 6

Swiss Rosti

1 onion
1 tablespoon olive oil
25 g (1 oz) butter
500 g (1 lb) small
    potatoes, peeled
salt and pepper

Fit the metal chopping blade and coarsely chop the onion. Heat the oil and butter in a shallow frying pan, add the onion and fry until soft.

Fit the slicing blade and slice the potatoes. Add to the pan with salt and pepper to taste. Mix with the onions, then press down firmly. Fry slowly until golden on the underside. Turn and cook the other side. Slide the rosti onto a warmed plate to serve.
Serves 4

Gratin Dauphinoise

50 g (2 oz) butter
750 g (1½ lb)
    potatoes
salt and pepper
125 g (4 oz)
    Cheddar cheese,
    grated*
1 egg
284 ml (½ pint)
    single cream

Use half the butter to thickly grease an ovenproof dish. Fit the slicing disc and slice the potatoes. Cover the base with a layer of potato. Sprinkle with salt, pepper and cheese. Repeat the layers, finishing with potato and reserving the last layer of cheese.

Whisk the egg and cream together. Pour over the top and dot with the remaining butter and cheese.

Bake in a preheated moderately hot oven, 190°C (375°F), Gas Mark 5, for 1 hour. If necessary, brown under a preheated grill. Serve immediately.
Serves 6

Indian Style Carrots

750 g (1½ lb) carrots
1 potato
50 g (2 oz) butter
2 teaspoons cumin
    powder
½ teaspoon chilli
    powder
1 teaspoon ground
    coriander
½ teaspoon turmeric
1 teaspoon salt
chopped coriander or
    parsley* to garnish

Fit the slicing disc and slice the carrots. Fit the metal chopping blade and coarsely chop the potato.

Melt the butter in a pan, add the carrot and potato and fry gently for 5 minutes. Add the spices, salt and 6 tablespoons water. Simmer, covered, for a further 7 minutes or until the water is absorbed. Serve immediately, sprinkled with coriander or parsley.
Serves 6

Courgette Flan

½ quantity shortcrust
  pastry (see page 14)
500 g (1 lb)
  courgettes
125 g (4 oz)
  Cheddar cheese
284 ml (½ pint)
  single cream
3 eggs
salt and pepper

Roll out the pastry and use to line a
25 cm (10 inch) flan tin. Bake blind in
a preheated moderately hot oven,
200°C (400°F), Gas Mark 6, for 10
minutes. Remove from the oven and
lower the temperature to 160°C
(325°F), Gas Mark 3.

Fit the slicing disc and slice the
courgettes. Arrange in the flan case.

Fit the metal chopping blade and
process the cheese. Add the cream,
eggs, and salt and pepper to taste to
the processor bowl and blend until
smooth. Pour over the courgettes.
Return to the oven and bake for 30 to
40 minutes, until set. Serve hot or
cold.
Serves 6

Celeriac, Mushroom and Bacon Salad

175 g (6 oz) celeriac
125 g (4 oz) mushrooms
125 g (4 oz) streaky bacon, derinded
2-3 parsley sprigs, chopped*
3 tablespoons natural yogurt
1 tablespoon lemon juice
1 tablespoon sunflower oil
1 teaspoon Dijon mustard
salt and pepper

Fit the grating disc and grate the celeriac. Fit the slicing disc and slice the mushrooms.

Grill or fry the bacon in its own fat until very crisp. Fit the metal chopping blade and chop the bacon.

Place the celeriac, mushrooms, bacon and parsley in a salad bowl.

Fit the metal blade. Put the remaining ingredients, with salt and pepper to taste, in the processor bowl, and process for 30 seconds. Pour this dressing over the salad and toss well to serve.

Serves 6

Leek, Cucumber and Tomato Salad

3 leeks
½ cucumber, peeled
250 g (8 oz)
  tomatoes, skinned
  and seeded
2-3 basil or parsley
  sprigs, chopped*
2 tablespoons French
  dressing

Fit the slicing disc and slice the leeks and cucumber.

Fit the metal chopping blade and chop the tomatoes for 3 to 5 seconds.

Place the vegetables in a salad bowl and sprinkle with the basil or parsley. Pour over the dressing and toss well to serve.

Serves 4

Fennel, Potato and Radish Salad

500 g (1 lb) new
  potatoes
salt
3 mint sprigs
1 fennel bulb
1 bunch of radishes
3 tablespoons French
  dressing

Cook the potatoes in their skins in boiling salted water, with one mint sprig added, for 15 to 20 minutes. Drain well.

Fit the slicing disc and slice the fennel, radishes and potatoes.

Strip the leaves from the remaining mint sprigs and chop, using the metal chopping blade.

Place the fennel, potatoes, radishes and mint in a salad bowl. Pour over the dressing while the potatoes are still warm and toss well.

Serves 4

Coleslaw with Peppers

175 g (6 oz) red
  cabbage
½ green pepper
½ red pepper
1 small onion
salt and pepper
6 tablespoons
  mayonnaise (see
  page 24)

Fit the slicing disc and slice the cabbage. Seed the peppers, cut in half lengthways, then slice.

Slice the onion, or chop coarsely using the metal chopping blade.

Place the vegetables in a salad bowl and season with salt and pepper to taste. Add the mayonnaise and stir well to combine.

Serves 4 to 6

MEAT, FISH & CHEESE DISHES

Curried Shrimp Pie

*¹/₃ quantity shortcrust
  pastry (see page 14)*
*50 g (2 oz) fresh
  breadcrumbs**
*2 teaspoons curry
  powder*
¹/₂ teaspoon salt
2 eggs
*300 ml (¹/₂ pint)
  milk*
*175 g (6 oz) peeled
  shrimps*

Roll out pastry on a floured surface.
Use to line a 20 cm (8 inch) flan tin.
Bake blind in a preheated moderately
hot oven, 200°C (400°F), Gas Mark 6,
for 10 minutes. Lower temperature to
160°C (325°F), Gas Mark 3.

Fit the metal chopping blade, place
the breadcrumbs, curry powder, salt,
eggs and milk in the processor bowl
and process until well blended.

Line the flan case with the shrimps
and pour over the curry mixture.
Return to the oven for 45 minutes,
until set and golden. Serve hot.
Serves 4

Monkfish Portuguaise

750 g (1½ lb)
  monkfish
500 g (1 lb)
  tomatoes, skinned
  and seeded
2 onions
1 red pepper, cored
  and seeded
2 tablespoons olive
  oil
½ teaspoon chilli
  powder
1 teaspoon salt
TO GARNISH:
lemon slices
chopped parsley*

Remove any bones from the monkfish, divide into 4 neat pieces and arrange in a greased ovenproof dish.

Fit the metal chopping blade and roughly chop the tomatoes, onions and red pepper. Add the oil, chilli powder and salt, mix well and pour over the fish.

Cover and cook in a preheated moderately hot oven, 190°C (375°F), Gas Mark 5, for 20 minutes. Remove the lid for the last 5 minutes.

Garnish with lemon slices and parsley to serve.
Serves 4

Haddock Quenelles

1 litre (1¾ pints)
    water
1 carrot, quartered
1 onion, quartered
1 bouquet garni
salt and white pepper
350 g (12 oz)
    haddock fillets,
    skinned
2 egg whites
142 ml (5 fl oz)
    double cream
TO SERVE:
Herb butter sauce (see
    page 29)
chopped chives*

Place the water, carrot, onion, bouquet garni, and salt and pepper to taste in a pan and simmer for 30 minutes.

Fit the metal chopping blade, place the haddock in the processor bowl, with salt and pepper to taste, and chop finely. With the processor running, gradually pour in the egg whites and cream until well blended and smooth. Shape the mixture into ovals, using 2 tablespoons, and place in a greased large shallow pan, leaving room for spreading.

Strain the hot vegetable stock over the quenelles. Cover and cook gently for about 10 minutes, until they are risen and firm. Drain thoroughly.

Pour over the Herb butter sauce and sprinkle with chives to serve.
Serves 4

Halibut Julienne

6 halibut steaks
2 tablespoons
   sunflower oil
salt and pepper
2 carrots
1 leek
2 celery sticks
50 g (2 oz) butter
2 tablespoons lemon
   juice

Brush the halibut steaks on both sides with the oil and season well with salt and pepper. Place under a preheated moderate grill and cook for 5 to 6 minutes on each side, until tender. Transfer to a warmed serving dish and keep warm.

Fit the grating disc and shred the carrot.

Fit the slicing disc and slice the leek and celery keeping them horizontal.

Melt the butter in a pan, add the vegetables and fry gently until soft. Add the lemon juice and simmer for 2 minutes.

Pour over the fish to serve.

Serves 6

Sesame Prawn Toasts

175 g (6 oz) shelled
  prawns
125 g (4 oz) haddock
  fillet, skinned
2 eggs
salt and pepper
4 slices white bread,
  crusts removed,
  toasted
4 tablespoons sesame
  seeds
oil for deep-frying
watercress sprigs to
  garnish

Fit the metal chopping blade, place the prawns, haddock, 1 egg, and salt and pepper to taste in the processor bowl and process until smooth. Spread evenly over the toast.

Beat the other egg and brush over the fish mixture, then press down onto the sesame seeds until evenly coated. Deep-fry each slice separately in hot oil for 2 minutes. Drain and cut into 8 to 12 fingers.

Serve warm, garnished with watercress.

Serves 4

Seafood Ravioli

PASTA:
250 g (8 oz) plain
  flour
1 teaspoon salt
2 eggs
1-2 teaspoons cold
  water to mix
FILLING:
1 × 198 g (7 oz) can
  tuna fish, drained
1 × 50 g (1¾ oz)
  can anchovies,
  drained
2-3 basil or parsley
  sprigs, chopped*
2 teaspoons grated
  lemon rind
salt and pepper
TO SERVE:
Tomato and orange
  sauce (see page 28)
  or 50 g (2 oz)
  butter
freshly grated
  Parmesan cheese*

Fit the metal chopping blade. Place the flour, salt and eggs in the processor bowl and process until the mixture forms a ball. Add a little cold water and process for 1 minute. Chill while preparing the filling.

Place the tuna fish and anchovies in the processor bowl and process until smooth. Transfer to a basin. Stir in the basil or parsley, lemon rind and plenty of salt and pepper.

Divide the pasta dough in half and roll out each piece to a rectangle 45 × 15 cm (18 × 6 inches). Put a rounded teaspoon of filling at 5 cm (2 inch) intervals on one piece. Brush edges and between the filling with water.

Carefully place the second piece of pasta dough over the top and press down between the filling and along the edges to seal. Cut between each round with a knife or pastry wheel.

Bring a large pan of salted water to the boil and drop in the ravioli, stirring to avoid sticking. Cook for 8 to 10 minutes, until al dente; drain.

Serve topped with butter or the tomato sauce and Parmesan.

Serves 4 to 6

Lebanese Lamb Patties

250 g (8 oz) bulgur
    wheat or cous-cous
500 g (1 lb) ground
    lamb
1 onion
1 teaspoon ground
    cinnamon
salt and pepper
oil for basting
SAUCE:
½ cucumber, peeled
    and cut into 2.5 cm
    (1 inch) pieces
150 g (5.2 oz)
    natural yogurt
TO GARNISH:
watercress sprigs

Soak the wheat or cous-cous in cold water for 1 hour. Strain and press out as much water as possible. Mix in a bowl with the lamb.

Fit the metal chopping blade and chop the onion very finely. Add to the meat with the cinnamon, and salt and pepper to taste and mix well. Process in batches until smooth.

Shape into 12 flat patties. Brush with oil and cook under a preheated moderate grill for 5 minutes on each side.

Meanwhile, process the cucumber and yogurt together using the metal chopping blade until smooth. Spoon into a serving bowl.

Serve the patties hot, garnished with watercress and accompanied by the sauce.
Serves 4

Leg of Lamb with Rosemary

1 kg (2 lb) potatoes,
    peeled
50 g (2 oz) butter
salt and pepper
2 kg (4½ lb) leg of
    lamb
2 cloves garlic, sliced
12 small rosemary
    sprigs

Fit the slicing disc and slice the potatoes.

Melt 40 g (1½ oz) of the butter in a roasting pan and add the potatoes. Season liberally with salt and pepper.

Rub the remaining butter over the surface of the meat. Make small slits at regular intervals over the top of the lamb and insert garlic and rosemary.

Place the lamb on a rack over the potatoes. Roast in a preheated moderately hot oven, 190°C (375°F), Gas Mark 5, for 1½ to 2 hours according to taste; the meat should preferably be pink inside. Turn the potatoes halfway through the cooking time. The herb-flavoured juices from the lamb give the potatoes a delicious flavour.

Serve the lamb with the potatoes, and courgettes or peas.
Serves 8

Lancashire Hot Pot

1 kg (2 lb) potatoes,
  peeled
2 onions
2 carrots
salt and pepper
4 lamb chump chops
4 lambs' kidneys,
  skinned, halved
  and cored
300 ml (½ pint)
  chicken stock
50 g (2 oz) butter

Fit the slicing disc and slice the potatoes; set aside. Fit the slicing disc and slice the onions and carrots separately.

Put a layer of potatoes in a casserole. Season well with salt and pepper. Arrange the chops and kidneys on top and cover with the onion. Season liberally. Cover with the carrots and pour over the chicken stock.

Arrange the remaining potato slices on top and dot with the butter. Cook in a preheated moderate oven, 160°C (325°F), Gas Mark 3, for 2 hours.
Serves 4

Steak Tartare

For those who like raw steak. Always choose a good quality lean steak and flavour it to your own taste.

*250 g (8 oz) fillet or
    rump steak or fillet
    of veal*
2 egg yolks
2 onions
4-5 small gherkins
2 tablespoons capers
4-6 parsley sprigs
TO SERVE:
salt and pepper
lemon wedges
Tabasco sauce

Fit the metal chopping blade, place the steak in the processor bowl and chop roughly. Divide in half, shape into 2 rounds and place in the centre of 2 serving plates. Make a well in the centre of each steak and drop in an egg yolk; alternatively, place the egg yolk in half an eggshell and arrange in the well.

Chop the remaining ingredients separately and arrange around the steak to serve; each person combines the ingredients to taste. Hand salt, pepper, lemon wedges and Tabasco sauce separately.
Serves 2

Beef Olives

8 slices topside of beef
50 g (2 oz) plain
    flour
2 tablespoons oil
2 onions
450 ml (¾ pint) beef
    stock
2 tablespoons tomato
    purée
STUFFING:
1 × 50 g (1¾ oz)
    can anchovy fillets,
    drained
50 g (2 oz) butter
2 teaspoons creamed
    horseradish
125 g (4 oz) fresh
    breadcrumbs*
2-3 parsley sprigs,
    chopped*
salt and pepper
1 egg, beaten
TO GARNISH:
chopped parsley*

First, prepare the stuffing. Fit the metal chopping blade, place the anchovies, butter and horseradish in the processor bowl and process until smooth. Place in a mixing bowl and add the breadcrumbs, parsley, and salt and pepper to taste. Bind together with the egg.

Divide into 8 portions and spread over the beef slices. Roll up and secure each with a wooden cocktail stick. Coat with the flour. Heat the oil in a pan, add the olives and brown all over. Transfer to a casserole. Coarsely chop the onion, add to the pan with any remaining flour and cook, stirring, for a few minutes. Gradually stir in the stock and the tomato purée and bring to the boil. Pour over the olives.

Cover and cook in a preheated moderate oven, 180°C (350°F), Gas Mark 4, for 1½ hours. Remove the cocktail sticks. Sprinkle with parsley to serve.
Serves 4

Bacon Crunchies

500 g (1 lb) streaky
   bacon, derinded
   (see note)
500 g (1 lb) potatoes
2 onions
50 g (2 oz) plain
   flour
1 egg, beaten
1 tablespoon brown
   sauce
1 teaspoon dried
   mixed herbs
salt and pepper
oil for shallow frying
watercress sprigs to
   garnish

Fit the metal chopping blade and
chop the bacon finely. Place in a
mixing bowl.

Fit the grating disc and grate the
potato and onions. Add to the bacon.

Add the remaining ingredients,
with salt and pepper to taste, and mix
well.

Heat the oil in a frying pan and
drop in spoonfuls of the mixture. Fry
for 8 minutes, turning once during
cooking. Drain on kitchen paper.

Serve immediately, garnished with
watercress.

Makes 16

NOTE: Inexpensive 'second cut' bacon
is ideal. Minced beef, lamb or veal
could be used instead of bacon.

Mumbled Eggs

This is a nineteenth-century dish which was originally eaten in gentlemen's clubs. It would now be best served for supper or a leisurely breakfast.

50 g (2 oz) button
   mushrooms
8 eggs
2 teaspoons made
   English mustard
salt and pepper
50 g (2 oz) butter
113 g (4 oz) cream
   cheese
2 tablespoons single
   cream
2 tablespoons
   chopped parsley*
   (optional)

Fit the metal chopping blade and chop the mushrooms. Add the eggs, mustard, and salt and pepper to taste to the bowl. Process for 5 seconds, or until the eggs are amalgamated.

Melt the butter in a pan, add the mushroom and egg mixture, and the cream cheese, and stir over a low heat until the eggs are set. Stir in the cream just before serving.

Sprinkle with parsley if preferred, and serve with buttered toast or warm rolls.
Serves 4

Stuffed Turkey Rolls

500 g (1 lb) boneless
   turkey breast
   slices
25 g (1 oz) white
   bread, crusts
   removed
2-3 parsley sprigs
1 onion
250 g (8 oz) pork
   sausage meat
125 g (4 oz)
   mushrooms
50 g (2 oz) butter
142 ml (5 fl oz)
   double cream
1 tablespoon brandy
salt and pepper
chopped parsley* to
   garnish

Beat out the turkey slices between
2 sheets of greaseproof paper.
   Fit the metal chopping blade and
process together the bread and
parsley. Add the onion, sausage
meat, and half the mushrooms and
process for 10 to 15 seconds.
   Divide between the turkey slices,
forming into sausage shapes. Roll up
the slices to enclose the stuffing and
fasten with wooden cocktail sticks.
   Chop the remaining mushrooms.
Melt the butter in a pan, add the
turkey rolls and mushrooms, cover
and cook gently for 30 minutes,
turning occasionally. Transfer rolls to
a warmed serving dish; keep warm.
   Add the cream, brandy, and salt
and pepper to taste to the pan and stir
until almost boiling. Pour over the
rolls and serve immediately,
garnished with parsley.
Serves 4

Spinach and Cheese Pasties

1 × 370 g (13 oz)
   packet frozen puff
   pastry, thawed
2 onions
2 tablespoons oil
1 kg (2 lb) fresh
   spinach, or
   1 × 227 g (8 oz)
   packet frozen
   spinach, thawed
227 g (8 oz) cottage
   cheese
1 teaspoon ground
   nutmeg
salt and pepper
beaten egg to glaze

Roll out the pastry thinly to a
rectangle 50 × 40 cm (20 × 16 inches)
and cut into 10 cm (4 inch) squares.
   Fit the metal chopping blade and
roughly chop the onions. Heat the oil
in a large pan, add the onion and fry
until soft. Add the spinach and cook
for 5 minutes.
   Transfer the spinach mixture to the
processor bowl and process for
10 seconds, then stir in the cheese,
nutmeg, and salt and pepper to taste.
   Put a tablespoon of filling on each
pastry square. Brush the edges with
water and fold over into triangles.
Brush with egg and make 2 cuts in
the top. Bake in a preheated hot oven,
220°C (425°F), Gas Mark 7, for
20 minutes, until golden. Serve hot.
Makes 20

Chinese Pork Balls

2 pork fillets, each
 weighing about
 250 g (8 oz)
2.5 cm (1 inch) piece
 root ginger, peeled
2 cloves garlic
1 × 227 g (8 oz) can
 water chestnuts,
 drained
salt and pepper
2 tablespoons soy sauce
1 teaspoon caster sugar
2 tablespoons oil
SAUCE:
4 tablespoons dry
 sherry
1 tablespoon tomato
 purée
1 tablespoon caster
 sugar
2 tablespoons white
 wine vinegar

Fit the metal chopping blade and
place the pork, ginger, garlic and
water chestnuts in the processor
bowl, seasoning with salt and pepper
to taste. Process for 15 to 20 seconds.

Add the soy sauce and sugar and
process for a further 2 seconds. Form
into small balls.

Heat the oil in a pan, add the meat
balls and fry for 10 minutes, until
crisp. Add the sauce ingredients to
the pan and stir until blended and
heated through. Serve hot.
Serves 4 to 6

Veal and Ham Pie

HOT WATERCRUST
PASTRY:
*350 g (12 oz) plain
flour*
1 teaspoon salt
*75 g (3 oz) unsalted
butter or lard*
*120 ml (4 fl oz)
water*
beaten egg to glaze
FILLING:
*750 g (1½ lb) pie
veal*
*250 g (8 oz) lean
bacon, derinded*
*1 cooking apple,
peeled and cored*
*1 teaspoon dried
mixed herbs*
2 tablespoons water
salt and pepper
JELLIED STOCK:
*2 teaspoons gelatine
dissolved in 300 ml
(½ pint) chicken
stock*

Fit the metal chopping blade, put the
flour and salt in the processor bowl
and process for 2 seconds to sift.

Place the fat and water in a small
pan and heat gently until the fat has
melted, then bring to the boil.
Immediately pour onto the flour with
the machine running. Process until
the pastry forms a ball. Wrap in cling
film and chill for 30 minutes.

Process the veal, bacon and apple
in batches and mix together in a bowl
with the herbs, water, and salt and
pepper to taste.

Cut off two thirds of the pastry,
knead lightly and roll out on a floured
surface to a 30 cm (12 inch) circle. Lift
carefully into a well greased 15 cm
(6 inch) loose-bottomed cake tin or
1½ litre (2½ pint) raised pie mould
and mould to fit the tin. Spoon in the
filling and brush the pastry edge with
water.

Roll out the remaining pastry for
the lid and place in position. Seal
well, trim and crimp the edges. Make
a hole in the centre of the lid and
decorate with leaves cut from the
trimmings. Brush with beaten egg.

Bake in a preheated hot oven,
220°C (425°F), Gas Mark 7, for
20 minutes. Lower the heat to 180°C
(350°F), Gas Mark 4, and bake for a
further 1½ hours. Leave to cool.

Gradually pour in the liquid jellied
stock through the hole in the lid.
Leave to cool, then chill until set.

Serve the raised pie cold, with
salads and relishes.

Serves 6 to 8

DESSERTS & PUDDINGS

Raspberry Cheese Dessert

750 g (1½ lb) fresh or
  frozen raspberries,
  thawed
75 g (3 oz) caster
  sugar
grated rind of 1 lemon
500 g (1 lb) skimmed
  milk soft cheese
4 tablespoons brandy
  or raspberry
  liqueur
6 mint sprigs

Fit the metal chopping blade, place
the raspberries in the processor bowl
with the sugar and lemon rind and
process to a purée. Set half on one side.

Add half of the cheese and brandy
or liqueur to the purée in the
processor and process until smooth.
Transfer to 3 individual glass dishes.
Repeat with the remaining
ingredients.

Garnish with the mint leaves to
serve.
Serves 6

Strawberry Mousse with Raspberry Sauce

500 g (1 lb) fresh or
  frozen strawberries,
  thawed
50 g (2 oz) caster
  sugar
4 tablespoons water
1 envelope gelatine
284 ml (½ pint)
  double cream
2 egg whites
TO SERVE:
Raspberry sauce (see
  page 26)

Fit the metal chopping blade, place the strawberries and sugar in the processor bowl and process to a purée.

Put the water in a small pan, sprinkle over the gelatine and heat gently until dissolved.

Pour the gelatine through the feed tube onto the purée with the machine running, then pour in the cream and blend well.

Whisk the egg whites and fold into the mixture. Pour into 6 individual moulds and chill until set.

Turn out onto plates and pour over the raspberry sauce to serve.

Serves 6

Pear Sorbet

4 dessert pears
150 ml (¼ pint)
    water
75 g (3 oz) sugar
white wine (optional
    – see method)
1 egg white
2 tablespoons grated
    chocolate*

Peel, quarter and core the pears. Place in a pan with the water and sugar and cook gently for about 10 minutes, until tender.

Fit the metal chopping blade, place the pears and syrup in the bowl and process to a purée. Make up to 600 ml (1 pint) with water or white wine. Pour into a rigid freezerproof container, cover, seal and freeze for 2 hours, until mushy.

Process again until smooth. Whisk the egg white, add to the bowl and process for 5 seconds.

Return to the freezer for 2 hours, then re-process and freeze until firm.

Transfer to the refrigerator 30 to 50 minutes before serving, to soften. Scoop into chilled glasses and sprinkle with the chocolate to serve.
Serves 4

Earl Grey Sorbet

A delicately flavoured sorbet which can be served as a dessert accompanied by biscuits, or as a 'refresher' between the starter and main course.

4 teaspoons Earl
    Grey tea
450 ml (¾ pint)
    boiling water
finely pared rind and
    juice of 1 lemon
75 g (3 oz) sugar
2 egg whites

Put the tea in a basin and pour over the boiling water. Add the lemon rind, juice and sugar. Leave until cold, then strain into a rigid freezer-proof container. Cover, seal and freeze for about 2 hours, until mushy.

Fit the metal chopping blade, place in the processor bowl and process until smooth. Whisk the egg whites until stiff, add to the bowl and process for 10 seconds.

Return to the freezer for 2 hours, then re-process and freeze until firm.

Transfer to the refrigerator 30 to 50 minutes before serving, to soften. Scoop into chilled glasses to serve.
Serves 4

Mango Fool

2 ripe mangoes,
    peeled
75 g (3 oz) caster
    sugar
284 ml (½ pint)
    double cream,
    whipped
25 g (1 oz) almonds,
    toasted, to decorate

Cut as much flesh as possible from each mango. Fit the metal chopping blade, place the mango flesh and sugar in the processor bowl and process until smooth. Add the cream and process for 5 seconds.

Spoon into glasses and chill. Top with toasted almonds to serve.
Serves 4

Frozen Apricot Mousse

*250 g (8 oz) dried
   apricots, soaked
   overnight in 450 ml
   (¾ pint) water*
3 eggs, separated
*75 g (3 oz) soft
   brown sugar*
*284 ml (½ pint)
   double cream,
   whipped*

Put the apricots in a pan with their soaking water and simmer for 15 to 20 minutes, until softened. Drain, reserving the liquid; cool slightly.

Fit the metal chopping blade, place the apricots in the processor bowl and process to a purée, adding a little of the cooking liquid if necessary.

Whisk the egg yolks and sugar until pale, add to the apricot purée and process for 10 seconds. Whisk the egg whites until stiff and fold into the mixture with the cream.

Pour into a 1.2 litre (2 pint) freezerproof bowl, cover, seal and freeze until firm.

Transfer to the refrigerator 30 to 50 minutes before serving to soften. Scoop into chilled dishes to serve.
Serves 6

Mint Chocolate Chip Ice Cream

3 eggs
75 g (3 oz) caster
   sugar
300 ml (½ pint)
   milk
284 ml (½ pint)
   double cream,
   whipped
3 tablespoons crème
   de menthe
50 g (2 oz) plain
   chocolate drops

Place the eggs and sugar in a heatproof bowl over a pan of simmering water and whisk until pale and frothy. Heat the milk to just below boiling point and pour onto the eggs. Continue stirring over hot water until thickened. Remove and cool.

Fold the cream into the custard, then stir in the liqueur. Pour into a rigid freezerproof container, cover, seal and freeze for 4 to 5 hours, until there is about 5 cm (2 inches) of solid ice cream around the sides.

Fit the metal chopping blade, place the ice cream in the processor bowl and process until soft. Add the chocolate drops and process for 5 to 10 seconds. Return to the freezer until firm.

Transfer to the refrigerator 30 to 50 minutes before serving, to soften. Scoop into chilled dishes to serve.
Serves 6
NOTE: Peppermint essence and a few drops of green food colouring may be used instead of the crème de menthe.

Franzipan Flan

1 quantity sweet flan
   pastry (see page
   15)
50 g (2 oz) cake
   crumbs*
1 × 411 g (14½ oz)
   can red cherries,
   drained and stoned
50 g (2 oz) butter
50 g (2 oz) caster
   sugar
1 egg
25 g (1 oz) plain
   flour
75 g (3 oz) ground
   almonds
1 teaspoon rosewater
   (optional)
1 tablespoon icing
   sugar, sifted

Roll out the pastry on a floured surface and use to line a 20 cm (8 inch) flan ring or tin. Bake blind in a preheated moderately hot oven, 200°C (400°F), Gas Mark 6, for 10 minutes. Lower the temperature to 180°C (350°F), Gas Mark 4.

Sprinkle the base with the cake crumbs and arrange the cherries on top.

Fit the metal chopping blade, place the remaining ingredients in the processor bowl and process until smooth. Spread over the cherries and return to the oven for 30 to 40 minutes, until firm to touch.

Sprinkle with the icing sugar and serve warm or cold.
Serves 6

Cherry and Almond Tart

1 quantity sweet flan
  pastry (see page 15)
50 g (2 oz) ground
  almonds
4-6 drops of almond
  essence
1 quantity Crème
  patissière (see page
  26)
500 g (1 lb) dessert
  cherries, halved
  and stoned
175 g (6 oz)
  redcurrant jelly
2 tablespoons water

Roll out the pastry on a floured surface and use to line a 20 cm (8 inch) flan tin or dish. Bake blind in a preheated moderately hot oven, 200°C (400°F), Gas Mark 6, for 20 minutes.

Stir the ground almonds and almond essence into the crème patissière and spread over the base of the flan. Arrange the cherries on top.

Place the redcurrant jelly and water in a small pan and heat gently, stirring, until the jelly dissolves. Brush over the cherries. Serve cold.

Serves 6

NOTE: Any fresh fruit in season, canned or frozen fruit, can be used instead of cherries.

18th Century Tart

½ quantity sweet
flan pastry (see
page 15)
75 g (3 oz) butter
75 g (3 oz) caster
sugar
4 egg yolks
25 g (1 oz) candied
peel
grated rind of
1 orange
1 dessert apple

Roll out the pastry on a floured surface and use to line an 18 cm (7 inch) flan ring or tin.

Fit the metal chopping blade, place the butter, sugar and egg yolks in the processor bowl and process until pale. Add the candied peel and orange rind and process for 5 seconds. Smooth over the pastry.

Fit the grating disc. Quarter, core and grate the apple (do not peel) and spoon over the flan. Bake in a preheated moderate oven, 180°C (350°F), Gas Mark 4, for 30 minutes. Serve warm or cold.
Serves 4

German Apple Pudding

125 g (4 oz) self-
raising flour
50 g (2 oz) soft
brown sugar
25 g (1 oz) ground
almonds
75 g (3 oz) butter
1 teaspoon lemon
juice
1 egg yolk
FILLING:
500 g (1 lb) cooking
apples, peeled and
cored
75 g (3 oz) soft
brown sugar
grated rind of 1 lemon
1 teaspoon lemon
juice
TOPPING:
50 g (2 oz) plain
flour
150 g (5 oz) soft
brown sugar
1 teaspoon ground
cinnamon
50 g (2 oz) butter

Fit the metal chopping blade and place the flour, sugar, ground almonds, butter, lemon juice and egg yolk in the processor bowl. Process until well mixed, then press into a greased 20 cm (8 inch) loose-bottomed cake tin.

Fit the slicing disc and slice the apples. Mix with the remaining filling ingredients and arrange over the sponge mixture.

Fit the metal chopping blade, place the topping ingredients in the processor bowl and process for 5 seconds. Sprinkle over the apples.

Bake in a preheated moderate oven, 180°C (350°F), Gas Mark 4, for 1 to 1¼ hours, until golden. Cool slightly, then carefully push out of the tin and slide onto a serving plate. Serve hot or cold.
Serves 4

Plum and Walnut Crumble

500 g (1 lb) plums,
    halved and stoned
75 g (3 oz)
    granulated sugar
175 g (6 oz) plain
    flour
75 g (3 oz) butter
75 g (3 oz) demerara
    sugar
125 g (4 oz) walnut
    pieces

Arrange the plums in a 1.2 litre (2 pint) ovenproof dish and sprinkle with the granulated sugar.

Fit the metal chopping blade, place the flour, butter and demerara sugar in the processor bowl and process for 15 seconds. Add the walnuts and process for 5 seconds.

Spoon the crumble over the fruit. Bake in a preheated moderate oven, 180°C (350°F), Gas Mark 4, for 30 to 40 minutes, until golden. Serve hot.

Serves 4

NOTE: Try other combinations: cherry and almonds, apples and mixed nuts, blackberry and hazelnuts.

CAKES, BREADS & PASTRIES

No-Cook Chocolate Cake

250 g (8 oz)
  digestive biscuits
125 g (4 oz) soft
  brown sugar
125 g (4 oz) butter
50 g (2 oz) raisins
3 tablespoons cocoa
  powder
1 egg, beaten
few drops vanilla
  essence

Fit the metal chopping blade and chop the biscuits coarsely.

Place the sugar and butter in a pan and heat gently until melted, then add the raisins and cocoa. Remove from the heat and add the egg and vanilla essence. Pour this mixture down the feed tube and process until well mixed.

Turn into a greased 18 cm (7 inch) sandwich tin and smooth the surface. Chill in the refrigerator until set.

Cut into wedges to serve.

Makes one 18 cm (7 inch) round
NOTE: Any broken plain biscuits are suitable for this recipe.

Sticky Gingerbread

300 g (10 oz) plain
 flour
1 teaspoon
 bicarbonate of soda
2 teaspoons ground
 ginger
2 teaspoons ground
 cinnamon
125 g (4 oz) soft
 brown sugar
125 g (4 oz) butter
175 g (6 oz) golden
 syrup
175 g (6 oz) black
 treacle
2 eggs, beaten
150 ml (¼ pint)
 water
2 pieces preserved
 ginger, sliced, to
 decorate

Fit the metal chopping blade and put the dry ingredients in the processor bowl.

Place the butter, syrup and treacle in a pan and heat gently until melted, then add the eggs and water.

With the motor running, pour the liquid ingredients down the feed tube and process until well mixed. Turn into a lined and greased 25 cm (10 inch) square cake tin and bake in a preheated moderate oven, 180°C (350°F), Gas Mark 4, for 40 to 45 minutes, until a skewer inserted into the centre comes out clean.

Transfer to a wire rack to cool. Cut into squares and put a slice of preserved ginger on each piece.
Makes 25

Royal Raisin Squares

¾ quantity basic
    shortcrust pastry
    (see page 14)
FILLING:
50 g (2 oz) cake
    crumbs*
175 g (6 oz) raisins
1 egg yolk
1 teaspoon finely
    grated lemon rind
TOPPING:
250 g (8 oz) icing
    sugar
1 egg white
1 teaspoon lemon
    juice
3 tablespoons
    redcurrant jelly

Roll out the pastry on a floured surface and use to line the base of a 20 cm (8 inch) square cake tin. Fit the metal chopping blade, put the filling ingredients in the processor bowl and process until blended. Spread over the pastry.

Fit the metal blade, place the icing sugar, egg white and lemon juice in the processor bowl and process until smooth. Pour over the filling.

Work the redcurrant jelly to a piping consistency in a bowl and spoon into a small piping bag fitted with a plain nozzle. Pipe a trellis design over the top of the cake.

Bake in a preheated moderately hot oven, 190°C (375°F), Gas Mark 5, for 30 minutes, then lower the temperature to 180°C (350°F), Gas Mark 4, and bake for 10 minutes. Cool on a wire rack. Cut into squares when cold.
Makes 16

Baked Cheesecake

50 g (2 oz) butter, melted
250 g (8 oz) digestive biscuits
227 g (8 oz) cottage cheese
200 g (7 oz) full fat soft cheese
125 g (4 oz) caster sugar
3 eggs, separated
25 g (1 oz) cornflour
½ teaspoon vanilla essence
142 ml (5 fl oz) soured cream

Fit the metal chopping blade and process the butter and biscuits together. Press onto the base of a well greased 20 cm (8 inch) loose-bottomed cake tin.

Place the cheeses in the processor bowl and process until blended. Add the remaining ingredients, except the egg whites, and process until blended. Whisk the egg whites until stiff and fold in.

Pour onto the biscuit base and bake in a preheated cool oven, 150°C (300°F), Gas Mark 2, for 1½ hours. Turn off the heat and leave the oven door ajar. Leave the cheesecake in the oven until cold.

Carefully push out of the tin and slide onto a serving plate.

Makes one 20 cm (8 inch) cake

Cinnamon Crumble Cake

125 g (4 oz) butter,
  softened
125 g (4 oz) soft
  brown sugar
2 eggs
50 g (2 oz) ground
  rice
125 g (4 oz) plain
  flour
1½ teaspoons baking
  powder
CRUMBLE:
50 g (2 oz) soft
  brown sugar
1 teaspoon cinnamon

Fit the metal chopping blade, put the butter and sugar in the processor bowl and process until pale.

Add the eggs one at a time with the machine switched on. Switch off the machine. Add the dry ingredients to the bowl through the feed tube and process for a few seconds to blend.

Turn into a greased 20 cm (8 inch) loose-bottomed cake tin and smooth the surface. Mix the crumble ingredients and sprinkle over the top.

Bake in a preheated moderate oven, 180°C (350°F), Gas Mark 4, for 35 to 45 minutes, until a skewer inserted into the centre comes out clean.

Leave in the tin until cold, then carefully push out and slide onto a serving plate.

Makes one 20 cm (8 inch) cake

Upside Down Cake

125 g (4 oz) butter
125 g (4 oz) soft
  brown sugar
2 eggs
125 g (4 oz) self-
  raising flour
TOPPING:
75 g (3 oz) butter
75 g (3 oz) soft
  brown sugar
1 × 439 g (15½ oz)
  can pineapple
  slices
4 glacé cherries,
  halved

First prepare the topping. Fit the metal chopping blade, put the butter and sugar in the processor bowl and process until pale. Spread over the base of 20 cm (8 inch) fixed-base cake tin. Drain the pineapple slices, reserving the syrup, and arrange on top. Place a cherry half in each ring.

Place the cake ingredients in the processor bowl, adding 2 tablespoons of the pineapple juice, and process until smooth. Spoon the mixture over the pineapple and bake in a preheated moderate oven, 180°C (350°F), Gas Mark 4, for 45 minutes, until firm. Transfer to a wire rack.

Serve warm or cold.

Makes one 20 cm (8 inch) cake

NOTE: This cake can be served as a dessert. Thicken the remaining pineapple juice with 1 teaspoon cornflour or arrowroot to make a sauce to serve with it.

Banana Cake

125 g (4 oz) butter,
    softened
175 g (6 oz) caster
    sugar
2 eggs
250 g (8 oz) self-
    raising flour
2 ripe bananas,
    roughly chopped
TO FINISH:
4 tablespoons lemon
    curd
2 firm bananas,
    sliced*
3 tablespoons lemon
    juice
125 g (4 oz) icing
    sugar, sifted

Fit the metal chopping blade, put all the cake ingredients in the processor bowl and process until smooth. Divide between 2 lined and greased 18 cm (7 inch) sandwich tins and bake in a preheated moderate oven, 180°C (350°F), Gas Mark 4, for 25 to 30 minutes. Turn onto a wire rack to cool.

Sandwich the cake together with the lemon curd and half of the banana slices. Sprinkle the remaining banana with 1 tablespoon lemon juice. Warm the remaining 2 tablespoons lemon juice and gradually mix into the icing sugar to make a smooth coating icing. Spread over the top of the cake and decorate with the banana slices.
Makes one 18 cm (7 inch) cake

Carrot and Pistachio Cake

2 eggs
1 teaspoon ground
  cardamom
125 g (4 oz) caster
  sugar
125 g (4 oz) butter,
  softened
250 g (8 oz) plain
  flour
1 teaspoon
  bicarbonate of soda
250 g (8 oz) carrots,
  finely grated*
50 g (2 oz) Pistachio
  nuts, chopped*
50 g (2 oz) ground
  almonds
125 g (4 oz) raisins

Fit the metal chopping blade, put the eggs, cardamom, sugar and butter in the processor bowl and process until smooth. Add the flour and bicarbonate of soda down the feed tube and process for 5 seconds. Add the remaining ingredients and process for 5 seconds or until well mixed.

Turn into a well greased 23 cm (9 inch) cake tin and bake in a preheated moderate oven, 180°C (350°F), Gas Mark 4, for 40 minutes. Transfer to a wire rack to cool.

Makes one 23 cm (9 inch) cake

Muscatel Cake

175 g (6 oz) butter, softened
175 g (6 oz) caster sugar
3 eggs
250 g (8 oz) plain flour
2 teaspoons baking powder
1½ tablespoons muscat wine
1 slice candied peel

Fit the metal chopping blade, put all ingredients, except the peel, in the processor bowl and process until combined and smooth.

Transfer to a greased 15 to 18 cm (6 to 7 inch) cake tin and place the slice of candied peel on top. Bake in a preheated moderate oven, 180°C (350°F), Gas Mark 4, for 1¼ hours. Leave in the tin for a few minutes, then turn onto a wire rack to cool.

Makes one 15 to 18 cm (6 to 7 inch) cake

NOTE: This is a Madeira-type cake, which keeps well. Madeira or marsala wine, or sweet sherry could be used instead of muscat wine.

Lemon Viennese Tarts

250 g (8 oz) butter,
  softened
75 g (3 oz) icing
  sugar
175 g (6 oz) plain
  flour
50 g (2 oz) cornflour
1 teaspoon finely
  grated lemon rind
TOPPING:
2 tablespoons icing
  sugar
2 tablespoons lemon
  curd

Fit the metal chopping blade, place the cake ingredients in the processor bowl and process until soft.

Put the mixture into a piping bag fitted with a 2.5 cm (1 inch) fluted nozzle and pipe into 12 paper cases, placed in a bun tin, using a circular movement.

Bake in a preheated moderate oven, 180°C (350°F), Gas Mark 4, for 20 minutes, until pale in colour. Transfer to a wire rack to cool.

Sift the icing sugar over the top and put a little lemon curd in the centre of each tart.
Makes 12

Treacle Tartlets

1/2 quantity basic
shortcrust pastry
(see page 14)
250 g (8 oz) golden
syrup
50 g (2 oz) fresh
breadcrumbs*
2 teaspoons lemon
juice

Roll out pastry on a floured surface and use to line a 12-hole deep bun tin.

Place the syrup in a pan and heat gently until melted, then stir in the breadcrumbs and lemon juice. Divide between the pastry cases and decorate with pastry trimmings.

Bake in a preheated hot oven, 200°C (400°F), Gas Mark 6, for 10 to 15 minutes. Serve warm or cold.
Makes 12

Danish Pastries

15 g (1/2 oz) dried
yeast
150 ml (1/4 pint)
warm milk
500 g (1 lb) plain
flour
300 g (10 oz) butter
50 g (2 oz) caster
sugar
2 eggs
FILLING:
50 g (2 oz) butter
50 g (2 oz) caster
sugar
50 g (2 oz) currants
2 teaspoons mixed
spice
TO FINISH:
250 g (8 oz) icing
sugar, sifted
2 tablespoons water

Soak the yeast in the milk for 10 minutes. Fit the metal chopping blade and put the flour, 50 g (2 oz) butter and the sugar in the processor bowl. Beat the eggs with the milk and yeast mixture and pour in through the feed tube. Process for 1 minute.

Roll out on a floured surface to an oblong 28 × 18 cm (11 × 7 inches). Put remaining butter, in a block, in the centre of the dough. Fold over top and bottom edges, give a quarter turn and roll out. Repeat turning and rolling 4 times. Cover and chill for 1 hour.

Meanwhile, prepare the filling. Place the butter and sugar in the processor bowl and process until smooth. Add the currants and mixed spice and process for 5 seconds.

Roll out the dough to 40 × 25 cm (16 × 10 inches) and spread with the filling to within 1 cm (1/2 inch) of the edges. Roll up from a long edge and cut into 12 slices.

Place on a greased baking sheet and leave to rise in a warm place for 20 minutes. Bake in a preheated hot oven, 220°C (425°F), Gas Mark 7, for 15 minutes. Cool on a wire rack.

Mix the icing sugar with the water. Spoon over each pastry while warm.
Makes 12

Malt Loaf

250 g (8 oz) self-
raising flour
25 g (1 oz) butter
25 g (1 oz) soft
brown sugar
150 ml (¼ pint)
milk
2 teaspoons black
treacle
1 rounded tablespoon
malt extract
50 g (2 oz) sultanas
GLAZE:
1 tablespoon sugar
2 tablespoons water

Fit the metal chopping blade and put the flour, butter and sugar in the processor bowl.

Warm the milk, treacle and malt extract, pour down the feed tube and process until smooth. Add the sultanas and process for 2 seconds.

Turn into a well greased 500 g (1 lb) loaf tin and bake in a preheated moderate oven, 160°C (325°F), Gas Mark 3, for 1 hour, until golden. Turn onto a wire rack.

Boil the sugar and water together and use to brush the top of the loaf immediately. Leave until cold, preferably until the next day. Serve sliced and buttered.

Makes one 500 g (1 lb) loaf

Sesame Baps

500 g (1 lb) plain
strong white flour
1 teaspoon salt
25 g (1 oz) white
cooking fat
15 g (½ oz) dried
yeast
1 teaspoon caster
sugar
150 ml (¼ pint)
milk
150 ml (¼ pint)
water
15 g (½ oz) sesame
seeds

Fit the metal chopping blade, put the flour, salt and fat in the processor bowl and process for 10 seconds.

Mix the yeast and sugar together in a small bowl. Warm the milk and water, pour over the yeast and leave for 10 minutes. Pour down the feed tube and process for 1 minute.

Transfer to a bowl, cover loosely with cling film and leave in a warm place for about 2 hours, until doubled in size.

Return to the processor and process for 1 minute. Divide into 12 pieces and knead lightly. Roll out slightly to flatten, place on baking sheets and leave to rise in a warm place for 20 minutes.

Brush with water or milk and sprinkle with sesame seeds. Bake in a preheated hot oven, 220°C (425°F), Gas Mark 7, for 15 minutes, until risen and golden. Cool on a wire rack.

Makes 12

Chapatis

250 g (8 oz)
    wholemeal flour
1 teaspoon salt
150 ml (¼ pint)
    water,
    approximately

Fit the metal chopping blade and place the flour, salt and water in the processor bowl. Process until a dough forms, then process for a further minute. Divide into 12 pieces, shape into balls and roll out thinly.

Grease a heavy-based frying pan and place over a moderate heat until hot. Add 1 or 2 chapatis and cook until brown underneath and blisters appear on the surface. Press down with a fish slice, turn over and cook the other side until lightly browned.

Cover and keep warm while cooking the remainder. Butter one side and serve hot.
Makes 12

INDEX

Acknowledgments

Photography by Paul Williams
Food prepared by Carole Handslip
Photographic stylist: Penny Markham